One More

Something destined this way comes
and I am running out of breath
trying to outrun my death.

There's still one more song to sing.
Another poem yet to write
before I enter heaven's light.

~ Candice James

Contents

Bend

Be loving.

Throw shiny pebbles
you've warmed in your hands
and held to your heart
into the sea of humanity.

Be kind.

Sail whispers
you've whetted with love
and laced with empathy
onto the winds of change.

Be willing.

Embrace with ease
all the sorrows
and joys you are given.
Surrender to the storms of life

Be the solidity of the stones
Be the lingering of the whispers
Be the supple branches of eternity

If you bend you will not break...

Bend.

Ever Changing

Inside a pocket of timeless time
I stood cloaked in white clover
invading the privacy of still waters
unstirred for centuries,
coveted pieces of breath
into shallow pools of blood
bringing life to the lungs of the universe
opening the lips of eternity
to form the word; and it was good;
and it became poetry;
and it became healing.

In the ever-changing pool of cosmic consciousness,
everything is a ripple effect. Everything begins with you.
Hold this thought gently in the calm of your mind.
The waves holding the image are flowing to your shore.
tide is yours to turn.

We are the creations, and the creators,
wrapped in the yin and yang of tumbling thoughts
and superconscious illusion, ever changing,
becoming reality.

Healing flourishes in silence.
Stand resolute in your own still, small silence!
Thrust your hand into your solar plexus
and grasp your creative force.
In one swift motion pull your hand out
and fling its contents skyward.
The sun, moon, and stars
will appear in sparkling array,
ever changing as you are ever changing.

As you will it...
so it will be.

Everything begins with you.

Something

There is an eternal mark on our souls:
　　　　a placement,
　　　a time and a tandem;

　Something of you that resides in me
and something of me that resides in you;
　　　Something that is,
　　　has always been
　　　and will ever be.

　　　There is no death in life
　　　　nor life in death;
　　　and yet they are both
　　　　continuously
　　　in constant overlap,
　　　　here and there
　　　in synchronous place
　　　　and time.

We cross through the here and there
unaware... yet aware on some level
　　that there is something:
　　present or absent,
　　current or past
that transcends everything
　into the eternal now.

Something that always is.

Something of you in me.
Something of me in you.
　　　Forever ...
wending its way home
　　　to us.

Now And Then

Time winks,
          creases and folds,
                    now and then.

On the white capped lip of an Ocean wave,
          the sun dances
          with diamonds
on a rippling turquoise mirror

          In this crystallized moment
clouds sigh through the puffed moist lips
          of a slow breathing sky

                    Gulls cry on high.
                    White doves centre,
                    then scatter in flight,
                    Bleached origami pillows
                    flung onto powder blue sheets

Somewhere,
          a lost dream,
          is winding its way home
                    Inside the Eternal Now.

                    Time winks,
          creases and folds,
now and then.

Tu Es Ergo Miraculum

Tu es ergo miraculum
You are the miracle.

Every second you are creating
a new physicality... unseen, unnoticed:
New skin cells growing
replacing dry brittle epidermis.
Dead strands of hair falling away.
Follicles bursting with new strands.
Internal cells replicating
into second generation, third generation
in lesser measures of their parent cell.
Ad letum. Ad infinitum.
This is the process of aging, part of our journey.

Every moment you are changing,
becoming the real you,
altering the pattern of your soul,
leaving your imprint on the world.
Speak with wisdom and honesty.
Allow your empathy full reign
as your path merges and weaves
through the lives of those you encounter.

Every day you have the chance:
To touch someone's heart,
To lift someone's spirit.
To make someone smile.

Making just one person smile can change the world.
Embrace each second, each moment

Smile...
Change the world today.

Tu es ergo miraculum.
You are the miracle.

Star-seed

We are star-seed.
Comet dust.
A universal sigh.
Connections dimensionalizing
in a parallax of infinite electricity.

We are electric,
Ascetic, eclectic.
Forgotten, remembered melodies
drifting through energy,
echoing songs
we write for each other.

We are frequency.
Sound everlasting.
Soothing, restless spirit
lifting the heavy heart.

The seen
and the unseen,
we have always been.

We are Star-seed.

Dance With the Surprises

Taste the mist of a shooting star.
Ride the surf on the milky-way.
Climb to the tip of a shimmering moonbeam
and slide down its highway of dreams.
Embrace the moment
and dance with the surprises.

Stop at the door with double locks.
Find the keys within yourself.
Stand at the edge of uncertainty.
Dive into the river of chance.
Embrace the moment
and dance with the surprises.

Listen to the whispering wind.
Walk through the echoes of the rain.
Swim in the sea of a pristine snowflake.
Rest in the palm of pastel rainbow.
Embrace the moment
and dance with the surprises.

Open up your heart and soul.
Keep your spirit flowing free.
Hear the universal rhythm
and when the music plays,
take the chance and dance.
Dance with the surprises.

Believe!

Believe in yourself!

Move with confidence
on the winds of change.
Embrace the unknown with certainty.

When one door closes
another one opens

Listen. Listen closely.
Hear the rhythm of the universe.
Embrace the moment.
Take the chance.
Step into the music
and learn a new dance.

Let the gentle thrum of your heartbeat
caress the inner core of your being
and turn the wounds of a lifetime
into beautiful scars,
trophies of trials overcome,
successes won through commitment
and unwavering endurance,
setting your spirit free
to be who you believe you are.

Look inward
that you may shine outward.

Living Fire

Born
from a wayward spark of dust,
we are the breath of dreams
becoming life.

We are fire
from the eternal cosmic flame.
Ablaze in the Eternal Now.
Breathing in unison
with our rising and falling chests,
our cresting and ebbing heartbeats,
lighting the wicks of our reveries,
illuminating the core of our soul.

We are embers
spilled from dust of stars.
Sparks bursting forth into flame
brilliantly lighting the days,
warming the edges of night,
peeling the black off the dark.

We are the spark.
We are the flame.
We are... living fire.

The Journey

The journey is one of encounters,
mysteries, joys and tears
filled with rivers and deserts
of emotions and feelings.

Standing outside the fire
we never feel the passion of the moment,
and the moment passes by overlooked.

The heart of the matter is
there are no guarantees
when it comes to matters of the heart;
but do not build walls around your spirit.
Keep the door to your soul
continuously ajar.
Some will walk past – a hurried journey;
Some will visit - a relaxed stop-over;
And some will take up permanent residence
Until your journey is ended.

Tears may fall
and hearts may break,
on the journey of a lifetime,
but all that truly matters
is the journey.

Poets' Dance

Hazy circles of possibilities
vibrate and float haphazardly touching down
onto the squares of quiet desperation
that invade every-day existence.

We remain unanswered questions
inside this massive silence
that holds all the answers.
> *All things pass away*
> *then come to pass again.*

Do not wait to step into the shadows of your soul;
The best part of you is beckoning you
to dive into the pristine white waters
of the poets' surreal dance:
where unfinished songs seeking completion
find their long-lost keys
and become seen and heard:
where liquid, quicksilver lightning
shakes the foundations of the mind
and rocks the questing heart
in the cradle of great expectations.

The wheel of fate keeps spinning toward you,
waiting for you to claim your dreams.
Follow the path of quills and ink stains
that penned the broken letters of death
onto the well-worn parchment of life.
> *All things pass away*
> *then come to pass again.*

We are all searching for the God particle,
quite unaware that we are the God Particle.

Look inward angel...
Step into the poets' dance!

Blessed Be The Rain

Blessed be the rain
that falls from the eyes in the sky.
There is a cleansing to this wet.
The fresh smell of soil and vegetation
escaping from the earth
infuse the atmosphere,
    sweeten the air.

Raindrops bump and grind
Falling in short lived expectation
Crowning invisible dominions
Holding court in nature's chambers
And disappearing mansions

Blessed be the rain
that falls from the eyes of the soul
filling the canyons of the mind,
overflowing the rivers of the heart
rinsing the spirit clean.

Blessed be the rain
keeper of raging rivers
and gentle streams
    The essence
of life and rebirth.

Blue Silence

In this slow grooved moment
of powder blue silence,
the glide of nature's paintbrush
and the whisper of the wind
are the only sounds we hear.

At the water's edge
a cold damp creeps into our feet,
winding itself up our legs
like an icy vine.

We rub our hands together
Thinking it may warm our legs
And hold the numbness at bay,
But the numbness continues to climb.

We begin a slow jog around the lake.
Fogged breath, blowing back in our face,
peppers the chilled air
making it bearable,
almost welcome.

As we jog
the lake whispers secrets to us;
and the wind blushes our cheeks
a rosier shade of red.

We are being painted
into nature's blue silence,
quite unaware
that we are ... the artists.

Bridges And Clouds

Twin tuning forks
reaching for the sky,
the suspension bridge
looks like the highway to heaven.
Clouds wrap their arms around her
in a lazy, hazy, impersonal embrace.
Chanting, whispering
in a windblown rush of hush.

Life is a bridge
peppered with clouds,
punctured with sunshine,
White moments unravelling
on an ebony pavement.

Life is a cloud
awash with bridges,
swaying on smiles,
teetering on tears;
a journey wet with wonder.

Bridges and clouds:
Sisters in solitaire;
Brothers in arms;
Chasing each other and us
on our inevitable journey
back to the stars.

Never Ending

In a breath never-ending,
on a wind ever bending,
these trees have always been.

Planning in the dark of a new moon,
before the light of day could find them,
these children of a lost forest god
were folding their branches in prayer,
when we lay down in their laps.

The morning dew still clung to their leaves,
shimmering like diamonds on display.
An eagle glided on high descending
with snow white feathered wingtip bending,
in salute to this pristine scene.

Walking through these forest canyons,
within this timeless chasm
of slow-motion unending changes
that mirror life and death,
we breathe a sweeter breath.

Tomorrow we'll travel on
until the trail meets
sand, beach, ocean and sky.

On a wave ever bending,
on a beach never ending
we'll merge with our shadows
and walk in the sun forever.

Mother

After I kiss your cheek,
I turn my cheek
as the tears shiver
rivers of aching pain
into my wrist and fingers.

I'm crying for you
and I'm crying for me.
So many years together
and yet, so much time apart.
You're flying away forever,
my beautiful bird,
leaving me behind.

A glint of silver,
shines on old memories,
sparkling, for a moment in time,
as did we
before our time was over.
Now, a new kind of loneliness.
More empty.

Not a day or night will pass by
when I don't think of you.
Not a smile or a tear will appear
without some image of you in it.
You'll always reflect in me
like a deeply rooted diamond,
dusted and powdered
with the sweet, salty, sugar
of yesterday's dreams.

And now...
I am orphaned;

but the mother and child reunion
is only a motion away...
only a motion away

Behind The One Way Mirror

They Live.
They do live on
in that other hazy dimension
just beyond our reach.

They walk.
They still walk
the canyons of our minds,
turning memories on and off,
in cinematic film clips of days
past, present and future.

They dance
to their own rhythm,
feathers
brushing against our being,
echoing...

> *'Remember me.'*
> *'Remember me.'*

They breathe
their presence into our souls
to fill the empty space
they left in us...
when they left us.

We live.
We do live on
behind this one-way mirror
just beyond their reach,

> *Waiting...*
> *Waiting...*

for the mirror to shatter.

In My Living Room

I saw my mother sitting in my living room;
and where she sat the room was aglow,
haloed in an amber aura.
I heard the uneven beat of her heart.

      Then

The atmosphere thickened.
Her shadow, stretched out before me,
began to diminish and fade.

Her ghost dissolved
into the thick of the atmosphere.

The exhaled breath of the night
composed her simple eulogy without words.

I saw my mother sitting in my living room
        and I knew ...
I knew she wasn't dead.

Remembering

Tonight
there is a remembering of things:

Hazy, forgotten,
but still living and breathing
in a veiled past.

Suddenly remembered
and savoured
like yesterday raindrops
a coveted
wet on the tongue
after a long, long drought.

Tonight
there is a spirit mood
invading my being on every level.
:

Remembering things forgotten;
remembering you
remembering me.

Remembering

Between the Thin Lines

The atmosphere thickens.
I see you walking toward me,
dimensionalizing into my realm.

I close my eyes for a minute; then open them
       and I see you moving closer
and reaching out to me

I close my eyes again, then open them
and I see you standing beside me.
       Close enough to touch,
       but still, just out of reach.

       And I don't know what to do...

       so I turn my head,
       the thick atmosphere dissolves
       and you fade from view

into the impermanence
between the thin lines
       of existence.

Fading Essence

In synch with the fading essence
of my perfume.
> I am half-asleep
> and half- awake,

> waiting for the gap between beats
> to grow longer, then longest,

> I wait and wait.
> half-asleep
> half-awake
> wrapped in this limitless silence;

> and I'm crossing over
> into ...
> the never-ending light

> in synch with the fading essence
> of my perfume,

.

When My Eyes Close

You turned my tarnished dreams
to gold inside your embrace.

      You were
the brightest star in my sky,
spilling dust on my heart to warm it.

The last time I saw you
I held your hand
and looked at you hard with love

I saw the story of my life
written in your eyes
before they closed.

   When my eyes close
       forever
I'll turn to gold again.

   At home at last
inside your embrace.

When the Falling Away Begins

When the falling away begins,
   what was is no more,
   and will never be again.

The falling away of leaves,
from the quivering tree branches:
      Releasing its children.
      as the falling away begins.

The falling away of rock
from the crumbling mountain ledge:
      Beginning its journey to transformation,
      as the falling away begins.

      When the falling away begins,
         what was is no more,

 On haunting days like these
  I feel the falling away begin
As I embrace my transformation.
   .

The God Particle

You are living consciousness,
            indestructible soul
                flowing through
the rivers of spirit's immortality.

You are not separate.

You move through
 the sands of time
as grains and atoms
  connected to

            the " I AM "
              and
  " THE GOD PARTICLE "

Shine

Stir your thoughts
with starlight at night,
Immerse the mystic in rays of pure moonglow
and gather them into a sequined scene.

Play the movie
on the synaptic screen
of your aching mind.

Follow the winding path less traveled
to enter the depth of the dream
you are dreaming.

Let your heartbeat echo
the rhythm of your footsteps.

Swim through the crimson river
to the essence of your creative spirit.

Polish the edge of your being
... and shine!

Majestic Silence

There is a magnetism to this silence,
a timeless tango
dancing to the whisper of a familiar song:

There is a flexibility to this magnetism:
Spinning.
Slow to rapid.

The same familiar song.
The same timeless face.

I always waltz with you
        through those lost hours
                in the warm hold
        of this majestic silence
                        until we meet again.

-

Just A Dream

All my days have been a dream
unravelling at its tattered seam,

I'm but a shadow in a dream.
I'm half awake but still asleep.

I watch the light of day elapse.
I see the dream I am collapse.

I stand unravelling at the seam
in this dream within a dream.

All my days have been a dream ...
                    just a dream.

We Drift And Dream

We are
>>> droplets of water,
>>> the dust of stars,
>>>>> the breath of angels.

We walk
>>> through a pretense of reality,
>>> trapped temporarily
inside the realm of unreality
>>> as the world spins and spins..

We are
>>>>> flakes of snow,
>>>>> shards of ice

>>>>> locked inside
>>>>> the hollow gasp
>>>>> of death's death,

>>>>>>> pirouetting,
>>>>>>> dancing
>>>>>> in and out of time
>>>>>> in a never-ending pool
>>>>>>> of timelessness.

We drift and dream,
>> again and again,
inside the dreams we create;
>>>>> inside the dream we are.

Heaven's Clock

Time passes.

The sky engulfs the horizon.
The night slowly drowns
in the dissolving moments
Of endless time.

I melt into myself
one last time
this side of heaven's clock.

Beneath her broken hands
and bruised faced
I stand in the clutch
of a relentless rain,
knowing deep in my heart
I'm leaving you behind...
but we'll only be parted a short time
until we embrace once more
on the other side of heaven's clock.

And Soon

And soon
    my heart will beat no more.
    and long I'll be gone from this world.
        Unseen in a realm of seen things.
    Unreal in the realm of reality.

When you see I'm gone,
    I'm not really gone.
    I'm right here beside you.
        Just a dimension away.
    Just a heartbeat away.

        So near.
        Yet so far.

And soon ...
    you'll see me again
    when you dimensionalize
    into the realm I am living in.

Scent

After your death

there was nothing left of you
for the longest while.

Time passed slowly
      And then
I imagined
      the sound
of your voice speaking to me;
      calling out my name
            from somewhere far, far away.

Sometimes,
      alone in an empty room,
          I suddenly smell
             The scent of your cologne.
          I scan the room
            for you
               but I am alone.

      Although you're not there
          I've come to realize ...
                  you are.

The Veil

There was an ambiance to the evening;
      an atmosphere,
      a thinly veiled succor,
      a glazed sweetness

      A summer rain
            fell from a pale blue sky
               of twilight dust.

There was an ambiance to the evening`
      thick with your imagined whispers
        and misty touch.
            ... I almost felt the veil dissolve.

Rapture

There always remains
at least one left over spark
        or ember
  one sweet left over memory
            to soothe a broken heart,
            to kiss the spirit's lips again
to romance the hands of time once more.

Wrapped in these special moments,
  I feel your breath on my cheek
        permeating the night
    into a comforting rapture
  that warms my soul to the bone.

Not Fade Away

Magnificence shone the night.
You stood in silver clothing.

You did not notice me standing there.
I tried to grasp your hand but it dissolved.

I saw you move your lips in silent words
before you disappeared into the haze.

Each time your ghost manifests
        your essence
is more real as it draws near.

Tonight I'll wait for you to reappear.
For magnificence to shine the night again
        that I may grasp your hand
            and it will not dissolve
            and you will not fade away.

Empty

I am empty

    A pale ghost

The sound of a song

    Faint echoes

A haunting rhythm

    His voice whispers
    through my falling tears

    Full of yesterday
    my heart is empty

A Ring Of Satin Water

A ring of satin water and sparkling stars
pull me into its magic
and the whisper of your voice
tugs at my heart
and sings me back home again.

Slice of Rain

I stand in a slice of rain
damp with yesterday's tears.

Blood and ink stans
Wash over my spirit
As the storms of life subside

Standing in this slice of rain
I am never alone...

God's grace is everywhere.

Indestructible

We, the remaining,
exchange:
Tears.
Sorrows.
Embraces.

You, the departed,
remain:
A footprint on life's water.
A ripple on the earth.
A whisper on the wind.
A tearstain on the ocean.
Indestructible.

Rest in peace
until we meet again.

Some Days

Some days
               I am afraid to die.
On these days
I am more careful,
      more alive,
             more extravagant.

Some days
               I am not afraid to die.
On these days
I am world weary,
      brow beaten,
             disenfranchised.

Some days are jeweled beaches.
Some days are damp gray sandbars.

      Days pass more quickly now
        than they did before.

Down to the Sea

I go down to the sea

I walk as fresh paint
brushing against breeze and tide
onto the canvas of time.

The ocean
spills into my eyes,
my heart and my soul.

You're gone but you're here.
I'm here but I'm there.
The real is surreal
and the surreal is real.

I go down to the sea
to balance my heart and soul;
to balance the here and hereafter.

I go down to the sea
to the lonely sea ...
where I always find you.

You Are Here

The gentle toss of the breeze
        through my hair
whispers kisses onto my cheek
as I picture you still here beside me.

It's unimaginable to think
you are not here,
so it must be true
that you really are here.

Sweet Prince of time and tides
        you roll in gently
on the shorelines of my mind
and I hold hands with your ghost.

You are here
with me always.

There is no death.

The Still

After the rending apart,
the cracking of the rose,
the wilting of the stone,
a bony finger
scratching at the soul clings.

Tears, still damp,
an immense stillness
creeps in.

In the echoed atmosphere
of the still,
a branch breaks.

De Profundis!
A teardrop falls.
A melody whispers...
and the dead dance.

Before The Stars Can Shine

I watch the evening sunset expire
in the chokehold of another dying day.

Dark honey drips
        from the flayed fingers of night
        blotting out the last remnants of light.

There is an inferred whimper,
                a muted whisper
        and a moment of total despair.

                But always ...
        always there must be darkness
        before the stars can shine.

Borderlands of Eternity

I carry yesterday's kisses
and wishes with me
in the fragile cradle of my heart.

I find I'm thinking of old days,
old friends, and old loves
that disappeared so quietly
but are not forgotten.

Sometimes I close my eyes.
Dreaming awake, I see their faces,
hear their voices
amidst a glow of music playing softly;
and I imagine I'm dancing again.

Daydreaming ...
here, but not really here

Soon all my yesterdays
will fade away.

I see the borderlands
of eternity now
and a new tomorrow
gently rolling in.

At Peace

A lone gull cries to the wind.
Windblown voices
and hazy dreams
lingering in the ether
whisper secrets
into the outstretched palms
of a grand magnificence.

I'm alone, but not alone.
I walk with angels
On the hallowed ground
of God's blue heaven
at peace at last.

Slowly Fading Away

Sometimes I hear voices and noises
        that nobody else hears
            and I wonder
                  if it's the other side
      reaching out to gather me into their fold.

Sometimes I smell a waft of perfume
          and I swear
      my mother is nearby.

Sometimes. I swear I glimpse a ghost,
        a fading grey shadow
        nudged into the corner of my eye.

These are passing things,
            slowly fading away ...
        as am I.

Fading Stardust

The ageless faces
of long-ago friends and lovers
     dance and romance
     the fading stardust
      in my eyes.

They parade through the shade
of my star dusted aging spirit
before they fade away.

I toast them as they dance on by
     and relish the last few sips
     of life's bittersweet wine:

One last look at the empty glass
     as the stardust
     in my eyes grows dim
     and I become
      eternal light.

Water and Rain

I long to go down to the shore again:
to hear the water speak to the rain,
to see the seagulls fly on high,
to hear the sadness in their cry.

The mast now hung with ragged sail
The long and winding path grows pale.
The sky-blue skies have turned to gray
and soon my soul will fly away.

An age-old stain on invisible suede,
the days of life begin to fade;
and I long to go down to the shore again
to hear the water speak to the rain ...

to hear the water speak to the rain.

December Heart

Through a crack in December's air
a winter song claws its way into my heart
and my night coils cold again.
An ice-clad moon sinks
behind the clouds in my eyes
in the dust-riddled gloom of the room.

My weary eyes
peer through the wrinkled lids

Through a crack in December's air,
night coils colder
around my December heart
inside this winter I can't escape.

But I know eternal spring
is only a motion away.

The Gap Between Pulse Beats

I understand the gap
between pulse beats.

This is the playground of ghosts
acting out dreams

There is a depth and pressure
and a razor's edge to twilight's glow.

I understand the gap
between pulse beats

This semi-death that has not yet been stretched.
This space in between feels no different
than the echo of the pulse.

When it stretches to infinity
we will know the full embrace of death
and we will see there is no difference
between life and death
but simply a long-exhaled breath
than never ends.

This is the place where death dies

I understand the gap
between pulse beats.

22nd Street Again

It's twilight time in the rain
at 22nd street again.

Somewhere there are golden sands
waiting on my pending footfalls.
Somewhere there are summer winds
beckoning me with soft calls.

And all the while I see your face
drifting through a sweet daydream.
And somewhere in the moving haze
the past unzips at the seam.

At a lonely bus stop in the rain
I wait to hold you once again.
I bide my time with bated breath
on this hazy side of death.

I'm pulled toward a soothing noise
drifting through the Ether tide;
then I hear your velvet voice
and suddenly you're at my side.

It's 22nd street again;
The dark and you and me and rain.
Love still hums its sweet refrain
inside yesterday's ink stain.

We stand on sparkling golden sands.
The time apart now in the past.
I kiss your face and hold your hands.
The world dissolves; I'm home at last.

The Book Re-Opens

Tides, coming full
yet waning and ebbing
on fading shorelines;
footsteps treading softly
leaving their imprint
on the pale blue iridescent dust
of ancient skylines
as the waters of life embrace us:

Years, ages, faces,
tears trading spaces
reverse through each other
spiralling the seasons
riding the rivers of life and death.

Windblown pages always moving,
                    forward,
              backward,
      opening, closing,
                       going past the end,
back to the beginning.

Through the pale iridescent dust of infinity.
Through the sparkling waters of eternity
onto the wheel of karma and rebirth:

A wink, a sanctified blink
and the book re-opens.:

A Dream In A Dream

I have laughed like water
    and cried like dust.
        I am least what I seem
        in this dying dream:
    an iron maiden turning to rust.

There are songs I will never play
    and words I will never write;
        music I will never hear
        until my angels reappear
    and slay this cold hard night.

Life's just a dream, in a dream,
    softly sighing and crying.
        an altar for smiles and tears.
        a platform for joys and fears.
    Just a dream in a dream that's dying.

    Just a dream
        in the dreams ...
    of the immortal dreamer,

A Distant Moaning

A distant moaning:
a silent song, a wordless rhyme,
drums whispering a broken lullaby beat.
The dead dance to their own music.
They dance to the songs only they can hear.,

A string of pearls.
A chain of golden silver.
A pendant of burnt amber.
A candle of sage and sienna.

These are the things
that remind me of the dead.

These are the things I will take to the dance
when I hear the distant moaning
and move slowly across
Time's river of tears
toward the dance of the dead.

A Matter of Punctuation

It comes down to a single moment
cloned from a bit of history
from a box inside a box, inside a box,
where my poems are layers of skin
hidden inside my bones.

The birds of silence have landed
with broken wings
and taken up residence inside
the ever-changing hours and minutes of my mind
where the seconds keep winding down
past the limits of the metronome
that has become my life.

I still have my words
and a vague memory of a haunting song
that plays like a rain dance
stolen from an indigenous dream.

I imagine the movements,
supple and static,
as I mime the names of the dead
for no reason at all except
to pay tribute and respect.

Tears punctuate my sentences
and form rivers in my story
as it heads toward the silence of the lake
I know awaits just around the bend;
and suddenly there it is.
The flowing story of my life
and the lake that holds
all my punctuated sentences.

And there it is ...
The end. Period.

The Understanding

We are knee-deep
in our own patterns of eternity
weaving the destiny we wear
mapping the world we create
stumbling through dreams,
tripping on nightmares,
cutting our teeth on the knife of life.

Visible and invisible,
peeling hours like oranges,
sharing slices of time,
we are ghosts
filtering in and out of sky and soil.

Dreaming ... we're lying awake.
Awake ... we're inside the dream.

We are the vapid expectations
of our own personal poetry
filling page upon page
with fog and sunlight,
moonglow and stardust.

Waist deep ...
we begin the understanding.

Songs of the Past

Oh for that last sweet draw of breath
        before I dance again with death
to those sweet, sweet songs of the past

I turn my ear to the quickening sound
of those sweet, sweet songs of the past
        softly calling me home.

        I reach out to clasp
    the welcoming hand of death
and softly whisper through glistening tears,
    take my breath away ...
            take my breath away.

In From The Cold

In the crystal mirror of my mind
I watch the dream I am unfold.

A distant bell is ringing,
a flock of angels singing.
I'm inside a living poem.
At last I'm finally coming home.

I'm sailing an outgoing tide
heading for the other side.
Again I'll hold hands with my soul
I'm coming in from the cold.

The Dance Begins

Shall we dance?
     I ask the shadows
     that haunt my dreams at night.

     I whisper to the wind
     and speak to the stars
          and then ...
          the music starts.

I let go of the last thread of life
               as it breaks ...
        then the music stops
     and the dance begins.

Pale Music

Pale music from the past
        fills every room in my mind.

           Voices from yesterday
      approach from all directions.

The full moon has fallen to its knees
        and broken the fragile string of life.

I am sinking into pale music:
        A sweet serenade
           sung by the voices of yesterday ...
        the voices I know so well.

A Rustle Of Ghost

In the drift and grift of a gray afternoon,
a rustle of ghost draws my attention.

> *It's so calm and serene,*
> *yet, otherworldly and eerie.*

The trees have fallen silent.
The world is almost asleep
but I keep vigil,
scanning the visible
for the invisible.

The dimming afternoon fades
then stops at the edge of the invisible
waiting patiently for me to follow
into the rustle of ghost ,,,
just beyond the gray.

Down to the Sea

I go down to the sea
to the lonely sea
where I know I'll find you.

I walk as fresh paint
brushing against breeze and tide
onto the canvas of time.

I listen to the spill of the ocean
as it tries to get into my eyes,
my heart and my soul.

You're gone but you're here.
I'm here but I'm there.
The real is surreal
and the surreal is real.

I go down to the sea
to balance my heart and soul;
to balance the here and hereafter

I go down to the sea
to the lonely sea ...
where I always find you.

I Am

I am the pale ghost of the night
flowing through cobblestone streets
unnoticed by the lovers
hiding in doorways
and under the bridges of time

I have become one
with a sky without borders
closing in on my fading shadow
absorbing my ethereal essence

The faraway echoes
of a timeless universe
pull at my hazy figure
as I drift above the cobblestone streets
      not certain if I am dead or alive,
        but certain that I am.

Awakening

On the river's pale pink sheen,
a long-lost dream skates by
losing an edge
on the wheel of time.

Awakening to a stir of echoes
this moment caves in on itself.

The liquidity of life disappears
into the set of stone
becoming spirit.

The All

In the flex and fluid flux
of inter-dimensional tectonic shifts
laid bare on opaque plates,
I glimpse a multiverse of realities
laying within the crease and fold
of the *"Eternal Now"*;
of the *"I Am"* and *"The All"*.

The bone shifters and spirit walkers
quantum leap and skydive through merging dimensions,
dissolving boundaries
on the diamond-studded rim of reality's wheel,
spoking through paths of possibilities,
dancing at the edge of dreams,
spinning them real
on the continuous weave of the loom
inside the *"Eternal Now"*.

Out-picturing myself from myself,
I rest in the curve of an angel's wing,
in tune with strange melodies...
Melodies that soothe the savage heart
and excite the spirit electric.

I dimensionalize
in cryptic silence
and golden hieroglyphs
into the vibrant hum of the universe
becoming the rhythm,
becoming the music,

Fully dimensionalizing
into the merging dimensions
of the *"I Am"*,
blending in surreal magnificence
into the whole
of *"The All"*.

The Edge Of The World

The music shakes, spills,
falls off the edge of the world
in muted tones and keys.

Moments slow, stop,
          collapse
into the eternal now.
Time ceases to exist.

> *Inside this vacuum:*
> *Silence within.*
> *Silence without.*

I move as wet hard mist
splashing, splintering, scattering
          above myself.
          below myself
     and yet within myself.

> I peer through
> a surreal foggy lens
> at familiar ghosts
> moving their lips
> beckoning me.

I perceive a whisper of wings,
A flutter of heartbeats.

> *Inside this vacuum:*
> *Silence within.*
> *Silence without.*

I fall off the edge of the world
     into the eternal now.

Invisible Dance

In the distance,
growing louder as it approaches,
a disembodied flute plays
in a harmony of circular echoes
held in invisible dance
nuzzling the rain
blowing kisses onto the wind
beckoning me to follow.

I walk through sun shadows,
mind strum rainbow songs,
sparkle for a brief moment,
held in invisible dance,
then melt into the sands of eternity.

In The Catch Of God's Breath

Beneath a sky of burnished gold
      beside a lake of diamond dust
I stand in awe of heaven's voice.

     Angels and cherubs circle above;
        I hear the voice of God
     calling to me from the other side
           inside the breath of death.

     A flurry of wings circles above
     and a hush falls over the silence.

     I become the silence
     between pulse beats;
alive in the catch of God's breath.

One Voice

My voice
is a chorus of rattling bones,
taut nerves
and distant dreams,

Liquid...
like slow moving water
over slick black rocks,
beneath timeless bridges,
pressing stone after pebble after stone
against my consciousness.

I am a shadow, a flicker,
interference patterns and sound waves
imprinted on the skin of infinity.

Thirsty for spirit, stars and knowledge
I dive into the deep,
Waiting ready for that stranger, death,
to embrace me,
crush my voice
through the dark heart of his lament
until we are both one voice
and my bones rattle ... no more.

The Blood Within The Bone

An angel shot silk
into the heart of the stars
and a universe was born.

The force behind the stone,
the blood within the bone
was the power of God,
creator of all.

He molds all life
and I am in his keep.

Upon my death
       I will not die.

The Waters of Time

The salt from the ocean
        nips at my eyes
scratching my spirit alive.

      I walk the waters of my soul
          on the shorelines of eternity

      The sun is a dying flamingo
          crashing into the distant horizon
      and I am slowly coming alive
          inside this dream I have died in

I move deeper into the waters of time
   to rock in the arms of the ocean
   and rest in the arms of the angels
that have always been calling me home.

Wild Wind

Walking the beach on a cold crisp morning
A damp sky above imposes a warning
Storm clouds droop in pale shades of gray
As a wild wind threatens to blow them away

I can feel the chill of second-hand breath
In this season of winter's impending death

I've been waiting and waiting
for what dreams may come
and wishing on falling stars,
coming undone.

So I throw off my coat on this cold crisp morning
Paying no attention to the sky's warning

Age has caught me and handcuffed my wrists.
My body's dissolving in teardrops and mists
Storm clouds rip open and drown the day
and the wild wind of death blows me away

The wild wind of death just blows me away.

Death

Death:

> A burning off of he body
> to leave the soul behind.
>
> The coming apart
> of Siamese twins.
>
> A painful release at best.

The final breath:

> A gasping eventide song
> sung with uncertainty.

Death:

> Our final freedom,
> crossed more frighteningly
> than thin cracking ice.

Amber Glow And White Light

In the dim of the sanctuary at midnight
the amber glow split into pristine white light.
In a rhythmic twist it moved into sound.
With a subconscious motion it scattered around.
The elegant air was singing in tune
at the star dusted edge of a glorious moon.

I knew it was time for my prayer to be heard
so I uttered it loud without saying a word.

In the dim sanctuary just past midnight
the amber glow split into pristine white light.
I entered heaven in the blink of an eye
And oh, oh ... what a beautiful sight ...
            oh what a beautiful sight.

The Dream Fulfilled

There's a shrine I visit in my mind.
When I'm lonely I go there to find
those who've passed on and left me alone
but still reside in my twilight zone.

Now day are short and nights are long.
I sleep inside an old lost song.
As time moves slow, I creep along
this path to home where I belong.

There's a special magic in the air
that fills my soul as I enter there.
I see past loves and family;
those who are so dear to me.

My breath's abating by and by.
The dream fulfilled; on wings I'll fly.
Wrapped inside a whisper and sigh,
I'll touch them in the blink of an eye.

Night's Beaujolais Wine

In the heartland glitter of sage and shine
night falls like dark red Beaujolais wine
hiding the beauty and scent of the rose.
The sky's eyes flutter then slowly close.

Beneath the sudden descent of darkness,
clouds fall to their knees and start to undress.
A sacred vibration awakens the sky
as throngs of angels slowly pass by.

Then the night's dark Beaujolais wine ebbs away
into the dawn of a sage and shine day.
The dew on the rose fades then disappears
as the sun reaches down to dry her tears.

Hazing above the horizon line
I flow in the wake of a smooth dry wine.
Swinging new songs I sway with the old
as the heat of the music abates and grows cold.

I stand in the quick of night's Beaujolais wine
in awe of God's grandeur and noble design.

Justified Water

Cleanse me in justified water.
Let ice cold needles puncture my heart
that i may die to myself;
then, resurrect me to walk again
in the brightest corner of light
where shadows flee and hide
from the truth chasing them down;
then send in the angels
to lighten my load
and clear the pathway ahead.

Let me stand justified
on the water you lay down before me.
Breathe your essence into me
that i may be you.
and see me through your eyes.

As I slowly sink into the justified water,
the water you laid down before me,
the last thing I see
is my waiting spirit
as I gently embrace the drowning.

Remembering the Rain

I remember the rain:
The texture of its touch;
And the timbre of its voice.

The rain speaks in soft staccato
to the evergreens;
it whispers to the gleaming
graffiti-carved park benches.

Here, the rain speaks in many languages and tongues:
In a loud, raspy voice to some.
In soft, gentle whispers to others.
And then it stops.

But its lips keep on moving

Mine stop and don't move again.

When I am dead
remember me...
remembering the rain.

The Only Moment
(written to artwork by M.K.Ciurlionis 1875-1910)

A broken winged lament
        has brought me to this moment,
        felled me to my soiled knees.

I can feel there is a golden tide of dreams
        just beyond my reach.
I can hear a flutter of wings above me
        just beyond my sight.

And just behind the shapeshifting clouds,
          I know eternity rests
       in the technicolour palm
of the creator's right hand.

With his left hand,
I can feel him lift his brush of many colours
        breathing life into death
           just beyond this realm.

In my mind
I can see him lifting my head
        and painting me into paradise
           just beyond this moment
      into ...
          the only moment
             that ever will matter.

Liquid Flame

A passionate moment in time
passes through itself
collapses into my soul.

A straw tinder box of abstractions
kindles itself into glorious flame
that burns in an orchestration
of deafening silences.

Inside the surreal breath
of this invisible rhythm
I embrace the ringing in my ears
and dance through a magical weave
of sparkling water and wine
in a strange familiar ceremony
of forgotten dreams
spinning real.

In the wake of distant thunder
the tinder box turns to ash.

An angel's wing grazes my soul;
the angel whispers my name
I turn to liquid flame.

Choose To Shine

Do not forget the spirit you are
   as you walk -
      through the dust
        of a distant star.

  In the slideshow of your life
     you are the star.

    Choose to shine.
   Illuminate the pathway
   for others to follow.

    Choose to shine!

QUOTES by Candice James

I Heard An Angel Whisper

I heard an angel whisper:
  'Always remember
 you are honest, pure
and a true child of God. '.
     'Trust in Him.
  He will always guide you
and clear the path before you.'

Spirit Everlasting

We are born from the light
     fade to black
       and then
    the pure illumination
   of spirit everlasting.

Only Love

    Unwrap the soul,
Peel back the layers of love
 and you will find the truth
       ... only love.

The Secret

Unfurl the flag in your heart
in the sweetest of sweet surrenders
and be true to your innermost self.
This is the secret
to divine happiness

Steps

We walk step by step.
The wise man heeds the silence
of the space
between steps.

Love

Love is all there is.
To utter the thought
there might be more
is a mortal sin.

Callings

There are callings,
and there are callings.
There are misguided dreams
and there are destinies.

They all whisper
in the same voice.
The wise man discerns
the different intonations.

Spirit

All is spirit,
in a state of continual flux,
shedding its dark disguise
thread by thread,
fabric by fabric,
body by body.

Poet Profile

Candice James, a poet, visual artist, musician, singer/songwriter, workshop facilitator and book reviewer. completed her 2nd three-year term as Poet Laureate of The City of New Westminster, BC CANADA in June 2016 and was appointed Poet Laureate Emerita in November 2016. Her credentials are: Board Advisor to Royal City Literary Arts Society; **Founder of**: Poetry New Westminster; Poetry In The Park; Poetic Justice, Slam Central and Royal City Literary Arts Society; **Past President of** Royal City Literary Arts Society; the Federation of British Columbia Writers. She is a member of the League of Canadian Poets, she has been keynote speaker at "Word On The Street", "Black Dot Roots Cultural Collective", "Write On The Beach" and has judged the "Pat Lowther Memorial Award" and "Jessamy Stursberg Youth Poet Award". She received Pandora's Collective Vancouver Citizenship Award; and the Bernie Legge Artist/Cultural award.

Candice has authored 24 books of poetry with 7 different publishers: "A Split In The Water" (Fiddlehead 1979); was the first book published and the most recent is The Depth of The Dance 2023.

Candice has featured at many venues both civic and public and appeared on television and radio. She has presented workshops, mentored writers; written prefaces and reviews, published articles, and short stories. Her poetry has appeared in many international anthologies and her poems have been translated into Arabic, Italian, Bengali, Farsi and Chinese. Her artwork has appeared in Duende Magazine and in the "Spotlight" at Goddard College of Fine Arts, Vermont, USA and her poetry inside and artwork ("Unmasked") on the cover of Survision Magazine, Dublin, Ireland and her poetry and artwork have appeared in Wax Poetry Art Magazine Canada. Many of her paintings have been used as book covers for authors nationally and internationally.

Website   www.candicejames.com

Printed in the USA
CPSIA information can be obtained
at www.ICGtesting.com
LVHW011907070224
770760LV00012B/76